EVERYDAY CHEMICALS

KATHRYN WHYMAN

Stargazer Books

New edition published in the United States in 2005 by:
Stargazer Books
c/o The Creative Company
123 South Broad Street
P.O. Box 227
Mankato, Minnesota 56002

Editor: Harriet Brown

Designer:
Pete Bennett – PBD

Picture Researcher:
Brian Hunter Smart

Illustrator: Louise Nevett

Printed in UAE

Library of Congress Cataloging-in-Publication Data

Whyman, Kathryn.
  Everyday chemicals / by Kathryn Whyman ;
  [illustrator, Louise Nevett].-- New ed.
    p. cm. -- (Science world)
  Includes index.
  ISBN 1-932799-23-0 (alk. paper)
  1. Chemistry--Juvenile literature.
  2. Chemicals--Juvenile literature. [1. Chemistry. 2.
  Chemicals.] I. Nevett, Louise, ill. II. Title. III. Science
  world (North Mankato, Minn.)

  QD35.W48 2004
  540—dc22   2003070754

CONTENTS

INTRODUCTION

Everything that exists—from the sun in the sky to the center of the earth, and from animals to vegetables—is made up of chemicals. Many of these are familiar to us, such as water, salt, sugar, iron, and oxygen. Chemicals can be different from each other in many ways. They have different tastes, like sugar and salt, or different appearances, like gold and silver. Chemicals come in many different forms; some are solids, others are liquids or gases.

Oil contains many different chemicals. It is extracted from deep within the earth.

In this book you will learn about the different physical and chemical properties of a range of substances. You will discover how a chemical can exist as a solid, liquid, or gas and find out that some substances are made of one or two chemicals, while others are made up of a large number. Find out how graphite in a pencil is actually made of the same chemical as a diamond and see how chemicals affect all aspects of our everyday lives.

Ice is made of chemicals.
It is the solid form of water.

THE CHEMICAL WORLD

Our world is composed of thousands of different substances. We call these substances "chemicals." Chemicals make up the air we breathe, the ground we walk on, and the food we eat. Even our bodies are a collection of chemicals!

Chemicals are often put into groups. Water, salt, sugar, and oxygen are all chemicals. We call them "natural" chemicals. Plastics, detergents, and cosmetics are everyday chemicals, too. But these do not occur naturally—they are "manmade." Both types of chemicals are useful. Manmade cleaning agents remove dirt from our clothes, and natural dyes from plants are used to color fabrics.

Water is made of chemicals and without it there would be no life on earth.

Our food contains many chemicals such as vitamins, proteins, fats, carbohydrates, and sugars. Chemicals give fruit and vegetables their color.

Wool and cotton can be dyed with manmade chemicals or natural chemicals from plants.

WHAT ARE CHEMICALS?

There are about 100 special chemicals called "elements." These are pure substances that cannot be broken down into simpler chemicals. The gases oxygen and hydrogen are both elements, so are iron and gold. Every element is made up of tiny particles called "atoms," that are much too small to see, even with a microscope. Oxygen is composed of oxygen atoms, iron is made up of iron atoms.

Atoms can join together to make "molecules." A molecule of an element is formed from only one type of atom. For example, oxygen exists as a molecule of two oxygen atoms joined together.

Combining chemicals

When two different elements combine, they often make a compound that is very different from either of them. The element sodium is a shiny metal. The element chlorine is a green and poisonous gas. Sodium atoms and chlorine atoms can combine to make a very familiar compound —salt! However, we do not make the salt we eat by combining sodium and chlorine. The photograph opposite shows salt being produced from sea water. In cooler countries, salt is mined from underground.

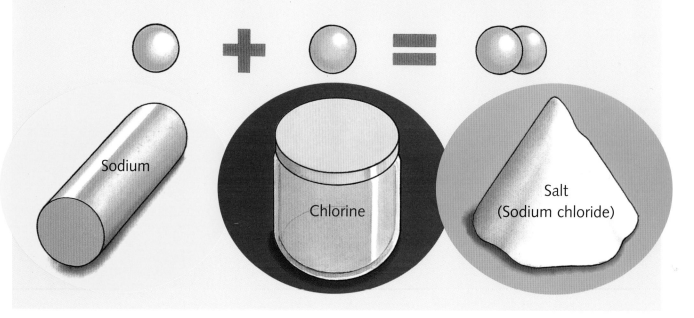

Sodium

Chlorine

Salt (Sodium chloride)

The atoms of one element may join together with the atoms of another element. When this happens, a completely different chemical is formed. For example, when two hydrogen atoms join with an oxygen atom, they make a molecule of water. Chemicals that are produced by combining two or more elements are known as "compounds." Water is a compound. Sugar, salt, plastics—in fact, most of the chemicals around us—are compounds. A compound usually has different characteristics from the elements from which it is made.

Plastic is a compound of many different elements.

The salt that we eat can be obtained from sea water.

SOLIDS, LIQUIDS, AND GASES

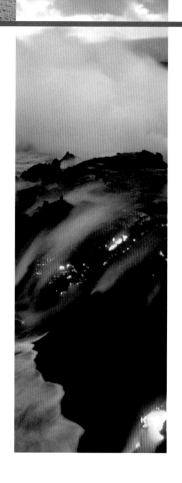

Chemicals may be solids, liquids, or gases. Water is a liquid. When water is cooled to below 32°F (0°C) it freezes and forms ice, a solid. When it is heated to 212°F (100°C) it boils and changes to steam, a gas. We say that water can change its "state."

A chemical's state depends on its temperature. Solids may turn to liquids and gases and then back to solids again, as the temperature rises and falls. We usually see metals and rocks in their solid state. When they're heated, they become softer. If they're heated to a high enough temperature, they melt and become liquid.

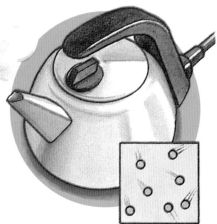

Ice
Because the molecules in a solid, such as ice, are held firmly together and can only move around a fixed point, they have a definite shape.

Water
As a liquid, water molecules can move around more freely. The "shape" of the water depends on the container.

Water vapor
The molecules in steam can move freely in all directions, spreading farther and farther apart until they fill their container.

In the Arctic, the temperature is so cold that sea water freezes into huge solid glaciers.

The water vapor molecules move freely in the steam given off by cooling towers.

CHEMICAL CHANGE

When water changes its state, its molecules are still made of hydrogen and oxygen—the chemical itself has not changed. When elements combine to make a compound, new molecules are formed. This is a "chemical change."

We see examples of compounds forming every day. Most metals combine with chemicals in the air. Copper roofs slowly turn green as the copper combines with water and oxygen to form a new compound. An iron nail left outside soon starts to turn brown. The iron has reacted with water and oxygen in the air to form "rust." Cars are made of several metals including iron. They have to be coated in paint to try to prevent them from rusting.

Baking a cake

When you bake a spongecake, one of the ingredients used is baking powder. As it is heated in the oven, the baking powder breaks down into different chemicals.

One of these is a gas—carbon dioxide. The bubbles of carbon dioxide throughout the sponge make it light and fluffy. The baked spongecake is now a new mixture of many different compounds.

Copper roofs turn green as the copper combines with oxygen to form a new compound.

Iron bridges need to be coated with chemicals to prevent them from rusting.

SOLUTIONS

Salt "disappears" in water. But a taste of the liquid tells you that the salt is still there. So what has happened to the salt? When salt is mixed with water, the sodium and chlorine atoms break away from each other and move freely in the water. Gradually, the sodium and chlorine atoms and the water molecules are mixed up evenly. The liquid is called a salt "solution." The salt has "dissolved."

Many substances dissolve in water. Water is a good "solvent." Carbon dioxide gas dissolves in water and makes it fizzy. Some substances dissolve in different solvents—paint dissolves in turpentine. Detergents "help" water to dissolve oil.

Drops of oil floating on water will rush away from a drop of detergent added to the water. This is because detergent causes the surface of the water to change and the oil starts to dissolve.

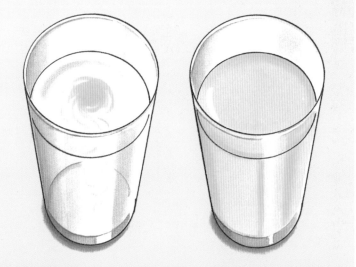

Diffusion

If orange juice is poured down a straw into a glass of water, an orange patch forms in the middle of the water. The molecules of the water and the orange juice are moving all the time. Eventually, the orange molecules spread evenly throughout the water and the solution looks pale orange all over. This spreading of molecules is called "diffusion."

Sea water is a massive solution of salt and water.

Oil-based paint does not dissolve in water, but it will dissolve in the solvent turpentine.

SEPARATING CHEMICALS

One way of separating chemicals is to use a "filter." A face mask is a type of filter. It is made of material that is full of tiny holes. Air can pass through these holes but particles of dust or paint are too big and get trapped on the outside of the mask.

A filter cannot separate salt from a salt solution. The sodium and chlorine atoms and the water molecules that form a salt solution are small enough to pass through the filter. However, if the solution is warmed, the water begins to change into vapor and, eventually, only salt is left behind. We call this process "evaporation." Stalagmites (shown right) form by evaporation.

Chromatography

There are three primary colors—red, blue, and yellow. Most inks are made by mixing two or more of these colors. To separate ink, a process called chromatography is used. To try this yourself, draw a small circle on blotting paper using a water-based pen. Then put a drop of water on top of the circle. As the water spreads through the blotting paper, it carries the chemicals at different speeds and separates the colors.

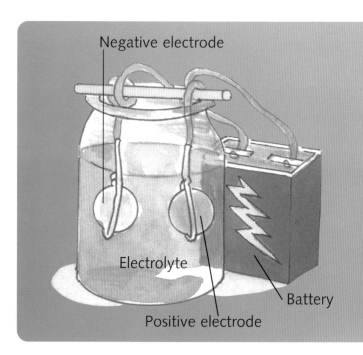

Negative electrode

Electrolyte

Positive electrode

Battery

Electrolysis

Electrolysis is a process used to separate elements from compounds. An electrical current from a battery is passed through a liquid—called the electrolyte. Some molecules in the electrolyte are positively charged and others are negatively charged. Positively charged particles are attracted to the negative electrode. Negatively charged particles are attracted to the positive electrode. The liquid begins to separate. Electrolysis can be used to purify metals.

Face masks separate chemicals by preventing large particles from passing through the holes.

CRYSTALS

We have seen how to separate salt from a salt solution. If you look at salt under a microscope, you can see that each grain of salt is a perfect cube. The cubes form naturally as the salt comes out of solution. They are called salt "crystals." All salt crystals are the same shape, but they may be different sizes.

Many chemicals form crystals. Sugar makes crystals and so does water when it turns to frost or snow. Each type of crystal has its own shape. Most rocks are made of crystals of chemical compounds called "minerals." Granite is made up of crystals of "quartz," "feldspar," and "mica." Crystals of diamond or emerald may be made into jewelry.

Salt crystals

Salt is made up of equal numbers of sodium and chlorine atoms. When salt is in solution, these atoms are far apart. But as the water evaporates, the atoms get closer together. They always arrange themselves in a "crystal lattice," giving salt its cubic shape.

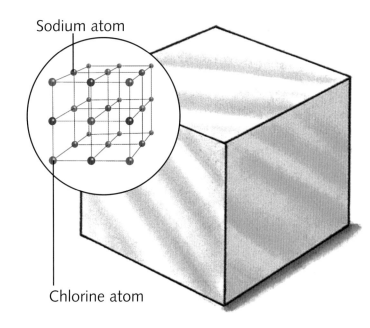

Water crystals can form beautiful patterns.

Sodium atom

Chlorine atom

Carbon

Carbon is an element: it is made up only of carbon atoms. But these atoms can arrange themselves in a number of ways to form several different types of carbon crystals. For example, charcoal is a soft black substance that can be used for drawing or burned as a fuel; graphite is harder and is used to make the "lead" in pencils. Surprisingly, diamonds are also pure carbon! Unlike charcoal and graphite, diamonds are extremely rare. They are used to make highly priced jewelry. Diamond is the hardest substance known and is used in industry as a cutting tool.

The graphite in a pencil is made of carbon crystals.

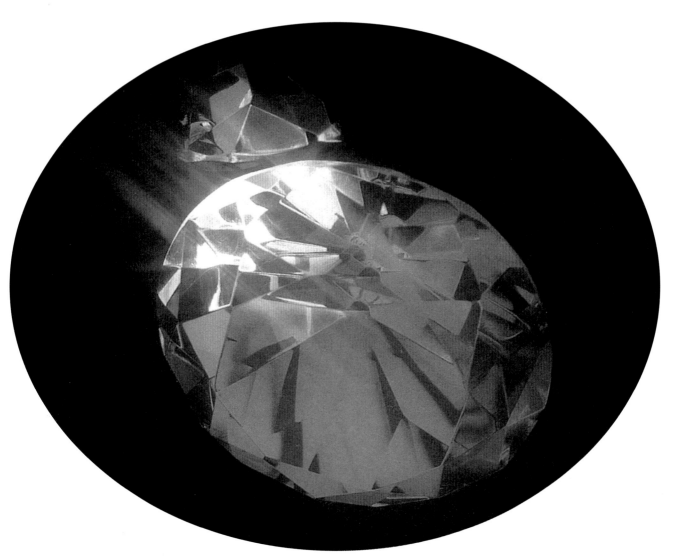

Diamonds, also crystals of carbon, are cut in a particular way to make them sparkle.

ACIDS AND ALKALIS

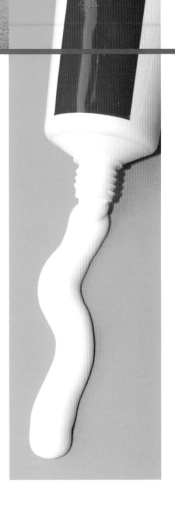

Some chemicals are acids or alkalis. Vinegar, lemon juice, and sour milk are all weak acids. They all have a similar sharp, sour taste. Oven cleanser, washing soda, and toothpaste are all alkalis. Alkalis taste bitter and feel soapy.

Our stomachs contain hydrochloric acid. This acid kills some of the bacteria in our food and helps us to digest our meals. Too much stomach acid causes indigestion. Medicines used to cure stomach pains are often alkalis. When you mix an alkali with an acid, you make a "neutral" solution—neither acidic nor alkaline. Many plants thrive in a soil that is not very acid, so farmers may add lime to the soil. Lime (an alkali) "neutralizes" acidic soil.

Acid rain, a form of polluted rain, is acidic enough to erode some stone statues.

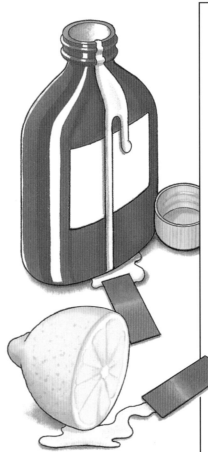

Indicators

An "indicator," such as litmus, is a substance that changes color when it is mixed with an acid or an alkali.

When litmus paper is dipped into lemon juice, it turns red. Alkaline stomach medicine turns it blue. When the acid and the alkali are mixed, a neutral solution is formed that does not color the litmus.

Car batteries contain a very strong acid solution. Never touch them with bare hands.

Farmers and gardeners use an alkali—lime—to neutralize acidic soil before planting.

CHEMICALS IN THE AIR

Air is a mixture. It contains many gases including nitrogen, oxygen, and carbon dioxide. Nitrogen combines with other elements to make compounds called "proteins." Proteins help plants and animals grow, and animals need oxygen to breathe. At the top of a mountain, there is less air than at the bottom. For this reason, mountain climbers sometimes need to take extra oxygen with them.

In sunlight, plants grow by combining carbon dioxide and water to produce more of the chemicals of which they are made. Gases in the air are being used all the time, but they never run out! The diagram below explains why.

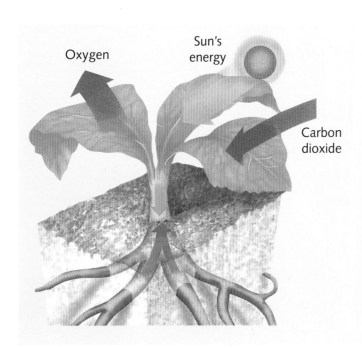

The Gas Cycle

We take oxygen from the air, but put back carbon dioxide. Plants take carbon dioxide from the air and, during the day, put back oxygen. Plant and animal bodies contain nitrogen. When they die, this nitrogen returns to the air or soil. Oxygen, carbon dioxide, and nitrogen are constantly recycled so that they never run out!

Fighter pilots have their own oxygen supply as there is very little air at high altitudes.

Plants and animals depend on each other to produce the chemicals needed for survival.

CHEMICALS FROM OIL

Crude oil is a thick, black liquid found deep under the earth's surface. It was formed millions of years ago from the bodies of tiny animals and plants that lived in the sea. Crude oil is a mixture of many very useful chemicals.

Crude oil is pumped up to the earth's surface and is piped to a refinery. Here, the different liquids are separated from each other. Some of the liquids, such as gasoline and kerosene, can be used as fuels. Others are changed chemically to produce compounds, such as plastics and waxes. Chemicals that come from oil are contained in many of the things we use every day, such as plastic bags and bottles, drain pipes, and some window frames and carpets.

Gasoline, the chemical used to power most cars, comes from crude oil.

Crude oil is found deep under the earth's surface and is then refined at the surface.

Distillation column

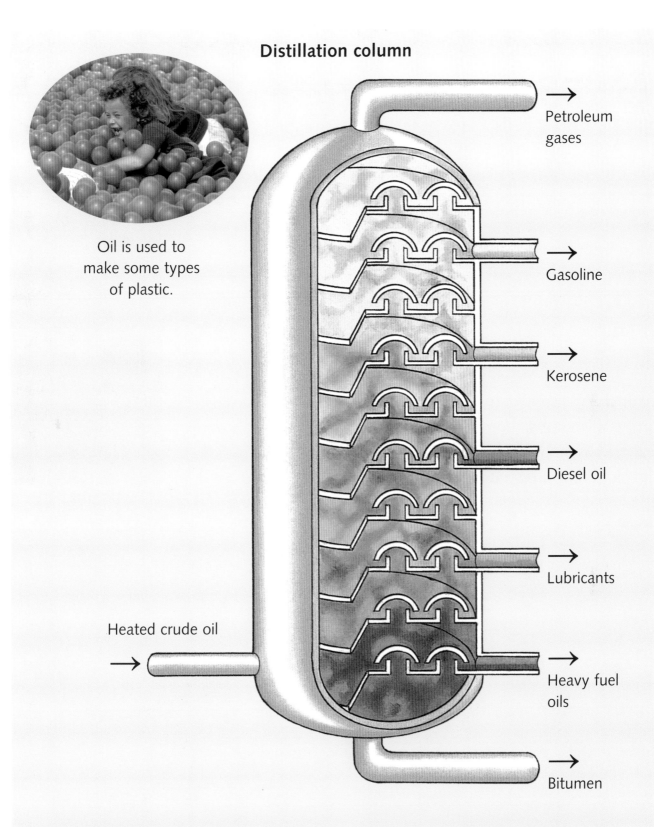

Oil is used to make some types of plastic.

→ Petroleum gases

→ Gasoline

→ Kerosene

→ Diesel oil

→ Lubricants

Heated crude oil →

→ Heavy fuel oils

→ Bitumen

Each liquid chemical boils at a different temperature. The temperature at which it boils is called its "boiling point." When crude oil is heated at the refinery, its temperature slowly rises. The liquid with the lowest boiling point is the first one to boil and form a gas.

This rises upward, then cools back to a liquid and is collected. As the heating continues, the liquids are separated and collected one by one. The last liquid to be collected is the one with the highest boiling point. This process of separation is called "distillation."

USES OF CHEMICALS

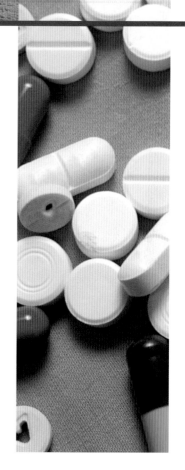

People have always used natural chemicals in their daily lives. Vegetable dyes are used to color wool and cloth, or to make paint. Other chemicals from plants have been used as medicines. Originally, drugs such as penicillin were made from molds grown naturally. Today, most of our medicines are produced artificially.

Scientists have produced chemicals to help farmers. Fertilizers, spread on the fields, make crops plentiful and strong. Pesticides can be used to kill insects that damage crops. Although chemicals are used to improve our lives, many may be harmful, too. For this reason, chemicals are developed and tested in laboratories before they are used.

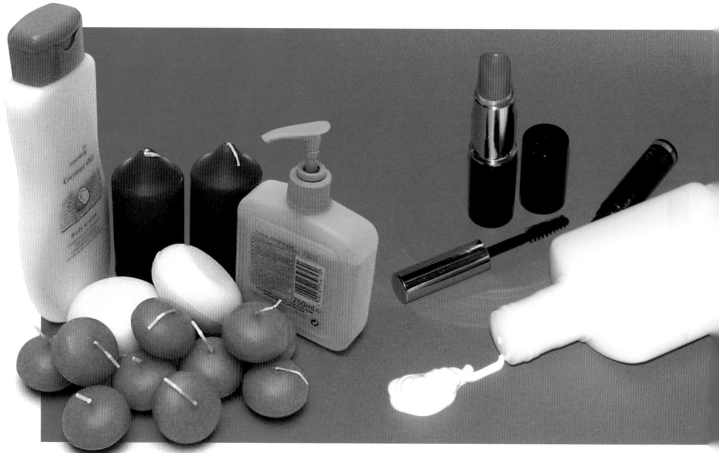

Everything we use is made of chemicals.

Pesticides are sprayed on crops to protect them from being eaten by insects.

MAKE YOUR OWN INDICATOR

Red cabbage contains a colored chemical that acts as an indicator. The blue dye from the cabbage turns pink in acids and green in alkalis. Neutral substances do not make the indicator change color. Make your own indicator and find out which of the everyday chemicals you have at home are acids or alkalis.

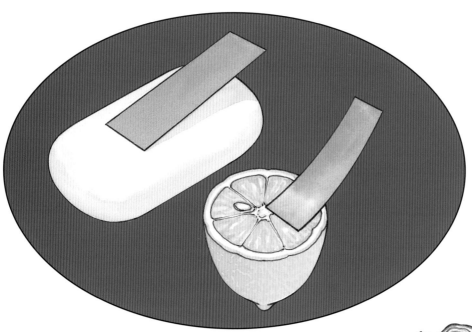

What you need
Red cabbage, a knife, a chopping board, boiling water, 2 bowls, blotting paper, a wooden spoon, clothespins, string, milk, soap, lemon juice, baking soda, and water

Ask an adult to boil some water and chop the cabbage leaves. Put the cabbage leaves in a bowl.

Carefully add the water to the cabbage leaves. Stir the mixture using a wooden spoon. The dye from the cabbage will turn the water blue.

When the solution has cooled, pour the water into another bowl. You don't need the cabbage leaves anymore.

Dip strips of white blotting paper into the indicator solution. When they are soaked in dye hang them up to dry using string, tied between two points, and some clothespins.

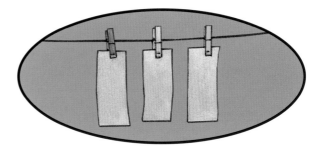

Use your indicator paper to test any liquids you may have. (You can also test solids dissolved in water). Just place a few drops of each chemical onto a fresh piece of indicator paper. Try testing chemicals such as soap, milk, lemon juice, and baking soda mixed with water. Different substances turn the paper different colors.

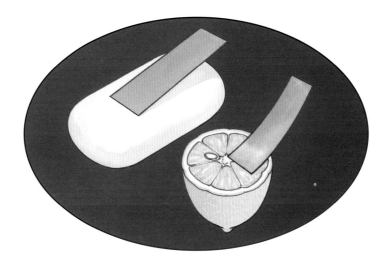

MORE ABOUT CHEMICALS

Chemicals surround us all the time and influence our lives without us even noticing. Here you can see a few more examples of some chemical and physical reactions with everyday chemicals.

Ask an adult to help you try some of them out for yourself.

Producing gas

Many different chemical reactions produce gas. At home, why not try producing carbon dioxide gas. To do this, mix together vinegar, which is acidic, and baking powder, which is alkaline, in a jar. Make sure the jar is in a sink—watch the bubbles of carbon dioxide erupt over the edge of the jar!

Physical change

If iron filings and sulfur are mixed together, the iron filings can be easily separated using a magnet. This is an example of a physical change, in which the material only changes its appearance. It is easy to reverse the change because no new substances are formed.

Chemical change

Eggs and bread are mixtures of compounds. When they are heated, new compounds are formed and a chemical reaction has taken place. We cannot undo this change in a simple way. Only complex chemical processes can reverse a chemical change.

How does evaporation work?

If a solution of salt and water is heated, the molecules move more rapidly. As the water boils, its molecules gain enough energy to fly off as gas. However, there's not enough energy for the salt to boil, and it is left behind.

GLOSSARY

Atom
A tiny particle. It is the smallest part of an element that can exist and still have all the characteristics of that element. It is the smallest unit of matter that can take part in a chemical change.

Compound
A substance consisting of two or more elements joined together. It cannot be broken down by physical changes.

Crystal lattice
The regular arrangement of atoms in a solid compound that gives it its characteristic shape.

Detergent
A substance that can be used to remove dirt and grease. Detergents are often manmade.

Diffusion
The gradual spreading of one material into another. Diffusion is quick in gases, slower in liquids, and very slow in solids.

Dye
A colored substance that can be firmly fixed to another substance. It cannot be removed by water or detergents.

Element
A substance that cannot be split into anything simpler by a chemical process, for example, iron or oxygen.

Erosion
The wearing down and breaking up of rocks by natural forces such as the wind, rain, ice, snow, and running water. Acid rain can erode stone statues.

Fertilizer
A substance containing chemicals that aid healthy plant growth.

Litmus
A dye obtained from a type of plant called a lichen. It acts as an indicator to tell if a substance is acidic, alkaline, or neutral.

Mixture
Two or more substances together that can be separated by simple physical means.

Molecule
Two or more atoms that exist as a group. A molecule is the smallest part of a compound that can exist on its own and still have all the characteristics of that compound.

Plastics
Compounds that contain carbon and whose molecules usually exist in long chains. These compounds often come from crude oil. Heat and/or pressure are involved in the manufacture of plastics.

Property
A characteristic that describes how a substance appears or behaves under certain conditions.

Reaction
The events that take place when two substances act on each other to produce new compounds.

Solution
When a substance dissolves in a liquid, we say it forms a solution.

Stalagmite
A column of calcium sulfate, usually seen growing up from the floor of a cave. Stalagmites are formed by a solution of water and calcium sulfate collecting on a surface. As the water evaporates, it leaves behind the calcium deposits.

INDEX

Photographic Credits

Abbreviations: l-left, r-right, b-bottom, t-top, c-center, m-middle

Front cover main, front cover mt, back cover main, 6b, 17b, 20bl, 23b, 26tr — Corbis. Front cover mb, 4tr — Corbis Royalty Free. 1, 7 main, 13t, 16tr, 18bl, 25tl, 27 — Corel. 2-3, 5tr, 10tr, 11t, 18tr, 22tr — Digital Stock. 4tl, 6tl, 8tl, 10tl, 12tl, 14tl, 16tl, 18tl, 20tl, 21b, 22tl, 24tl, 26tl, 28tl, 30t, 31t, 32t — John Deere. 4-5, 11b, 12tr, 24b — Photodisc. 6tr, 24tr — Ingram Publishing. 7 inset, 28tr — USDA. 8tr, 21t, 26bl, 26br — Select Pictures. 9b — Bruce Coleman. 9tr, 13b — Flat Earth. 14tr — Rexam plc. 15t — Stockbyte. 15b — Brian Hunter Smart. 19b — Zefa. 20tr — PBD. 23t — US Air Force.